REDDITCH
AND
THE NEEDLE DISTRICT
IN OLD PHOTOGRAPHS

REDDITCH

THE LOVERS' WALK

REDDITCH

AND
THE NEEDLE DISTRICT
IN OLD PHOTOGRAPHS

COLLECTED BY
RAYMOND J. SAUNDERS

ALAN SUTTON

Alan Sutton Publishing Limited
Phoenix Mill · Far Thrupp · Stroud · Gloucestershire

First published 1991

British Library Cataloguing in Publication Data

Redditch and the Needle District in old photographs.
I. Saunders, Raymond J., *1930–*
942.443

ISBN 0-86299-953-7

With much love to Eleanor, Sarah and Jennifer

Typeset in 9/10 Korinna.
Typesetting and origination by
Alan Sutton Publishing Limited.
Printed in Great Britain by
The Bath Press, Avon.

CONTENTS

FOXLYDIATE, near Redditch, c. 1905, looking towards Bromsgrove with the old Fox and Goose public house on the middle right of the picture. This hostelry was demolished in the 1930s and replaced in 1938 with the Foxlydiate Hotel, then an ultra modern public house.

INTRODUCTION

Redditch lies fourteen miles south of Birmingham, in the heart of England, in the County of Hereford and Worcester. In 1964, it was designated a 'new town', by Sir Keith Joseph, to relieve overcrowding in Birmingham and the West Midland conurbation. Since then a new town centre has been created, miles and miles of roads have been constructed, thousands of trees have been planted, and the population has more than doubled.

People from all over the British Isles have come to live and work in the new town of Redditch. Some stay a short time and move on, others are putting down roots, adopting this area of the Midlands as their long-term home. How do they see their town? Probably as a busy conurbation with a space-age Kingfisher Centre, with large noisy shops in malls and paved pedestrian streets. They travel on miles and miles of new highways, perhaps work on one of the purpose-built industrial areas, and live in one of the hundreds of new homes on a landscaped estate.

Redditch, however, has a fascinating history. The land on which it stands once lay in the shadow of the Royal Oak Forest of Feckenham. Bordesley Abbey, established by Cistercian monks, was the centre of commerce from 1138 until its dissolution in 1538. Until the turn of the century Redditch, internationally renowned for needle making, was a small country town, very dependent on its satellite needle-making communities in villages like Studley, Headless Cross, Crabbs Cross and Astwood Bank. As well as needle making, and the fishing tackle industry, the area spawned famous companies, such as Herbert Terry and Sons and the Royal Enfield Cycle and Motor Cycle Company.

The photographs in this book, many previously unpublished, depict the area before the coming of the new town. It is not meant to be a written history book, but a many-faceted pictorial view of life as it was, covering topics from sport to transport, theatre to religion, murder to parades, and fashions of the day.

Hopefully this book will help the people of 'old Redditch' to re-live good memories and evoke talking points, and for those new to the town, give them a taste of Redditch as it was when life was lived at a slower pace.

I have always lived in the area, and have always had a particular interest in the history of the town, collecting together many items, postcards, programmes, cuttings, etc. depicting the life and times of the people of Redditch.

Listed below are the commercial photographers of the district between 1890 and 1940. The studio addresses are given when known and they are in Redditch unless otherwise stated.

J. Boreham, Astwood Bank • A. Harold Clarke
H.E. Coles (late Fox & Co.), Victoria Buildings, Evesham Street
Charles Evans, Graphic Studio, 6 Alcester Street
Q.H. Fountain, 109 Evesham Street • J.H. Fox & Co., Unicorn Hill
Graham & Co., Alcester Street • A. Green • T. Hamblett
J. (Joe) Harman, 83 Lodge Road • R. Hodges, Evesham Street
E.A. Hodges, 1 Evesham Street • C. Hodges, Astwood Bank • John Hensman
R.S. Hill, Graphic Studio, 2 Alcester Street • A.D. Lewis
Lewis Brothers, 2 Alcester Street • Regal Studios, Evesham Street
The Regent Studio, 109 Evesham Street
L.L. Sealey, Beoley Road and Other Road • Sherwoods, Photographic Studios
W.H. Smith, High Street, Alcester • Walter Terry, 91 Evesham Street
J.J.G. Whitehouse

A TYPICAL 'HOLIDAY' CARD, c.1911.

SECTION ONE

Views of Redditch

CHAPEL GREEN, REDDITCH.
From the Brow of Fish Hill

CHAPEL GREEN, an artist's view showing the distinctive cupola on the roof. This chapel was replaced in 1855 by St Stephen's church.

ST STEPHEN'S CHURCH, C.1904, the parish church of Redditch.

ST STEPHEN'S CHURCH, 1960. The area around St Stephen's church has changed very little during the last thirty years.

THE KIOSK, a bandstand unveiled by Mrs R.S. Bartlett on 15 May 1883. The iron railings and gates were melted down as part of the war effort during the Second World War, otherwise little has changed.

REDDITCH INSTITUTE, Church Green West, c.1893. The Smallwood Hospital was built in 1895 on the site of these shops and cottages.

Institute and Hospital, Redditch

REDDITCH INSTITUTE AND SMALLWOOD HOSPITAL, c.1920.

SMALLWOOD HOSPITAL. The hospital was opened in 1895 by Lord and Lady Windsor of Hewell Grange. Austen Chamberlain MP also attended the ceremony.

PROSPECT HILL, c.1912. This is the view from the spire of St Stephen's church, looking down the hill.

CHURCH GREEN AND THE CORNER OF CHURCH ROAD. This is now the site of Birmingham Midshires Building Society offices. Notice the postman and the telegraph boy.

CHURCH GREEN WEST, c.1923, with the original Redditch Building Society offices on the right in the foreground, and a bus-stand in the centre of the picture.

THE PARADE and St Stephen's church, c.1950.

THE PARADE. The first building on the left of the picture was the Gas Board offices and showroom.

THE PARADE, looking towards Evesham Street, c.1923. A shady place to sit and chat on a sunny afternoon.

THE INSTITUTE, HOSPITAL AND BANDSTAND across the gardens of Church Green.

ST STEPHEN'S CHURCH, c.1904.

EVESHAM STREET, c.1905. Plenty of shoppers are around to pose for the camera, although one appears to be more interested in his 'penny dreadful'. The shop of E.A. Hodges, Stationer, the publisher of this card, can be seen next to James Huins, a shoe shop.

THE SOUTH END OF EVESHAM STREET, looking towards the church, c.1949.

EVESHAM STREET with very few people and just one horse-drawn vehicle on this particular day, c.1900. The Talbot public house replaced the Vine Inn seen on the left of the picture, but the shops on the right remained little changed until the coming of the new town.

THE PARADE AND CHURCH GREEN from Evesham Street. A policeman was required at the crossroads until traffic lights were installed.

MARKET PLACE in the early 1950s.

ALCESTER STREET. The premises of J. Scott and Son, Friendly House, Tailors and Outfitters, in the right foreground of this picture is now the site of Redditch Public Library.

MARKET PLACE and St Stephen's church, c.1905.

IPSLEY GREEN in the early 1900s, looking down towards the needle and fish hook factory of H. Milward and Sons. There seems to be a chimney fire in the house next to the Methodist chapel.

THE JUNCTION OF IPSLEY STREET AND MILLSBOROUGH ROAD, looking towards Mount Pleasant, in this early photograph taken c.1898. The Baptist chapel on the left of the picture was demolished and the site developed to become the main factory of Herbert Terry and Sons Ltd.

BAPTIST CHAPEL, Ipsley Green. The Jubilee Oak was planted in the foreground to commemorate the jubilee year of Queen Victoria.

LOOKING DOWN IPSLEY STREET from the junction with Lodge Road towards Ipsley Green.

THE OLD ROUNDHOUSE, a needle mill, and the cottage were built in 1799 by Charles Avery for the Sheward Brothers. The round-house was an experimental wind-powered needle mill. It was commercially unsuccessful and was demolished in 1892.

THE OLD ROUNDHOUSE from an early watercolour. This was probably painted earlier than the photograph taken on the opposite page. Notice the bricked-up windows on the photograph, and the difference in the chimneys. It was situated in Mount Pleasant, now the site of a garage.

ST GEORGE'S CHURCH, c.1900.

MOUNT CARMEL ROMAN CATHOLIC CHURCH, Beoley Road, c.1904.

A TURNPIKE TOLL-HOUSE once stood in Mount Pleasant, opposite where the Park Inn now stands.

MOUNT PLEASANT, c.1906, looking towards Headless Cross with Baker's Pork Butchers shop on the right of the picture.

MOUNT PLEASANT, c.1906, looking towards Redditch town centre with the Plough and Harrow public house, which is now the Redditch Liberal Club, in the far distance.

MOUNT PLEASANT in the snow. This type of card was used as an advertisement by E.A. Hodges who produced the card.

BATES HILL METHODIST CHURCH, and the minister's house, c.1921.

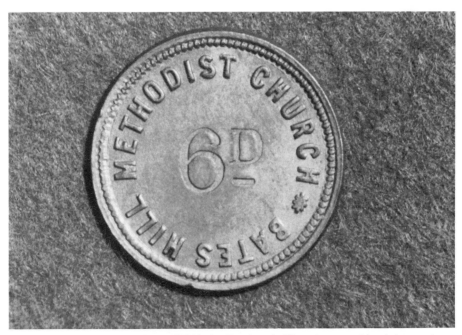

A SIXPENNY TOKEN issued by Bates Hill Methodist church. The tokens could only be used at a church function or put into the collection plate.

A HORSE AND CART crossing the River Arrow ford on Beoley Road. The milkman with his churn on wheels has stopped to chat with the ladies.

THE FORD IN FLOOD when few vehicles would attempt to cross.

BEOLEY ROAD, looking towards the town centre. The Cricketer's Arms public house is on the far right of the picture, and the vehicle in the foreground is a night-soil cart.

A HERALDIC CARD OF BROMSGROVE ROAD, c.1906, by E.A. Hodges.

OAKLEY ROAD, C.1930, looking towards the junction with Ludlow Road.

PAPER MILL WALK AND POND, Beoley Road, C.1920.

REDDITCH RAILWAY STATION'S FORECOURT and the bridge over the railway line leading to Bromsgrove Road, c.1900.

A LEAFY BROMSGROVE ROAD, c.1906.

OSWALD STREET, c.1905, when children were able to play quite safely in the road.

THE NORTH END OF PLYMOUTH ROAD with the railway embankment on the left.

HEWELL ROAD. The view has changed very little since 1908 when this photograph was taken.

EASEMORE ROAD where the absence of motor traffic allows these ladies to push their perambulators up the middle of the road.

CLIVE AVENUE is now known as Birmingham Road. This photograph was taken looking towards the town centre.

Three Arch Bridge, Redditch.

THREE ARCH BRIDGE carrying the Redditch-Birmingham railway line over Windsor Road.

BROCKHILL LANE, c.1923, at the junction of Salters Lane and Hewell Road.

RECTORY ROAD has changed little over the years except that it is no longer a through road.

THE BIRMINGHAM–REDDITCH–PERSHORE TURNPIKE TOLL-HOUSE built in 1825, and known locally as Granny Locks. It was located on Birmingham Road at the junction with Dagnell End Lane.

THE PALACE THEATRE, Alcester Street, on its completion in 1913.

BUILT BY THE SAME BENEFACTORS of the Smallwood Hospital, William and Edwin Smallwood, these almshouses were for the old and needy of the town.

A TYPICAL POSTCARD showing various scenes around Redditch.

SECTION TWO

Trade and Commerce

MAKING NEEDLES in 1764: figure 1, the cutter; figure 2, the piercer; figure 3, the clearer; figure 4, the flatter; figure 5, the temperer; figure 6, the baker; figure 7, the pointer, dresser, etc.; figure 8, the polisher.

FORGE MILL, now restored as a working museum.

HENRY MILWARD JP, 1840, the founder of the Milward Needle and Fishing Tackle Co.

AERIAL VIEW, C. 1922, of the Milward needle and fishing tackle factory with St Georges Road in the background.

THE FASHIONS of the 1920s are very well displayed here by the ladies of the Works Committee of H. Milward and Sons.

In 1698 the first "Double Century" Needles were made at Redditch

IN two hundred years, methods of manufacture have altered but the quality remains. To-day, as ever, "Double Century" needles are the finest obtainable.

Our unequalled experience has taught us how to make the best. You will appreciate the quality. It always pays to buy the best.

Let us send full particulars.

JAMES SMITH & SON
(Redditch) Ltd.,
Astwood Bank, Redditch.

Makers of: "Double Century" Knitting Pins "Apex" Hat-pins, "Apex" Gramophone Needles.

A VICTORIAN ADVERTISEMENT for the local product, c.1898.

A GROUP OF NEEDLE WORKERS outside the factory of William Woodfield of Elm Road, Redditch. Note the button boots.

THE WORLD'S LARGEST FISHING TACKLE MANUFACTURERS, S. Allcock & Co. Ltd. The factory was built in 1866, but extended and modernized after a fire in 1920.

BAKERS AT WORK around seventy years ago in the bakehouse of Webb and Sons, Church Green and Peakman Street.

MR ROBERT WALKER SMITH M.I.MECH.E., Managing Director of the Enfield Cycle Co. Ltd, c.1923.

AERIAL VIEW of The Royal Enfield Cycle and Motor Cycle Works, Hewell Road, in an almost rural setting.

LODGE FARM can be seen beyond the Britannia Batteries factory.

A DISASTROUS FIRE on 12 September 1940 left part of the Britannia Batteries factory, Union Street, in ruins.

THE CENTENARY YEAR OF HERBERT TERRY AND SONS was in 1955 and their head office on Ipsley Green was decorated for the occasion.

HERBERT TERRY, founder of the firm Herbert Terry and Sons.

CHARLES TERRY JP CC, who took over from his father and was for many years managing director of the firm.

A HOME-MADE CAR, made in 1907 by a local man, Fred Harris, who later emigrated to New Zealand. The inscription on the back of this photograph reads, 'with a Chater LEA 8 hp engine, friction transmission, six speeds and reverse, electric lights, and body made from galvanised iron'.

GARAGE AND SHOWROOMS OF ALBERT A. PITTS, 50, 52 and 54 Evesham Street, c.1922.

W.H. SMITH'S GARAGE in Evesham Street.

MR FRANK MILLS standing in the doorway of his cycle repair shop on Bates Hill.

MR J. DUGGINS AND FAMILY posing outside their grocery and provisions store in Beoley Road, c.1900.

AN ARTIST'S IMPRESSION OF THE ORIGINAL UNICORN HOTEL, with a grocer and tea dealer occupying part of the building.

DEPARTMENT STORE OF F.W. HOLLINGTON AND CO. LTD, Evesham Street in 1922.

A WELL-STOCKED WINDOW DISPLAY by E.G. Harmer, Ladies and Children's outfitters, The Parade, Church Green, just after the First World War.

THE GENTLEMAN'S OUTFITTERS SHOP OF G.F. BROUGH,
11 Evesham Street, c.1922.

A READY-MONEY DRAPER. J.R. Sage kept this shop on Bates Hill, and it is now The Fisherman's Catch.

THE MILLINERY SHOP OF MRS HELEN PARSONS on The Parade, c.1923.

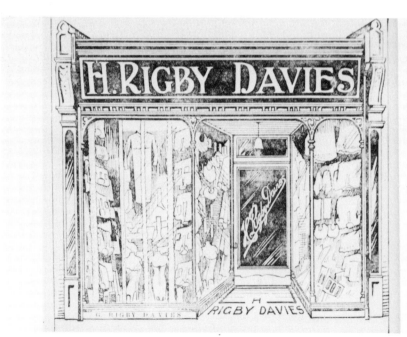

GENERAL AND FANCY DRAPER, Mrs H. Rigby Davies, Evesham Street, c.1920.

THE WINDOWS OF J. SCOTT AND SON, Tailors and Drapers of Market Place, could certainly not display much more.

THE PREMISES OF HARRY B. TARLETON in 1923, Builder and Contractor of Church Green East. This building now houses the offices of Robert Cartwright, Estate Agents, and the *Redditch Advertiser*. The archway on the left of the picture is known as Gorton's Arch.

ARTICLES OF CLOTHING were displayed outside the shop as well as in the windows of Geo. Heaphy and Sons, 2 and 4 New Street.

THE TABLES ARE SET in the café owned by E.L. Watkins at 13 Evesham Street, c.1922. Note the fresh flowers.

CRANMORE, SIMMONS AND CO. LTD, House Furnishers and Ironmongers, c.1920. The Yorkshire Bank and Income Tax offices now occupy this prime site.

TOKEN issued by the Kings Arms Hotel Bowling Club.

THREEPENNY TOKEN of the Earl of Plymouth Friendly Society. These tokens were issued by various establishments as change or in lieu of goods. They could only be used with the named company.

A CHEQUE of the Redditch branch of the Birmingham Banking Co., dated 10 December 1888.

THE MAIN POST OFFICE OF RED-
DITCH, Church Road, c.1904.

THE CUSTOM-BUILT OFFICES OF THE REDDITCH BUILDING SOCIETY, completed in 1922 at a cost of
five thousand pounds. Now known as the Birmingham Midshires Building Society, it is on
the same site although much modernized.

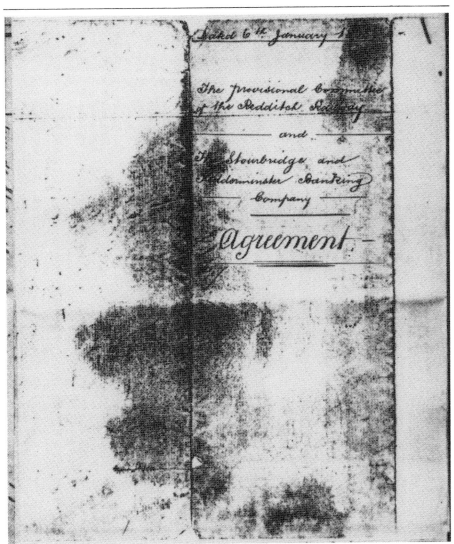

A COPY OF AN AGREEMENT between the Provisional Committee of the Redditch Railway and the Stourbridge and Kidderminster Banking Co., c.1859. The majority of the original promoters of the railway were customers of this local bank.

Redditch Bank.

LIABILITIES.		ASSETS.	
Customers' Accounts		Cash	
Discounts		Bank Notes	
Commission, &c.		Sundries	
		Own Notes	
		Stourbridge Bank	
		Bills	
		Suspense Account	
		General Charges	
		Purchase of Premises	
		Furniture Account	
		Stamps	

REDDITCH BRANCH BALANCE SHEET for 30 June 1862 for the Stourbridge and Kidderminster Banking Co. (forerunner of the Midland Bank).

THE LICENSEE AND HIS FAMILY outside their public house, the Cricketer's Arms, Beoley Road.
From left to right: Ralph, Ena, Mr Edwards, Bert, Osmond, Mrs Edwards, Dolly.

CRICKETER'S ARMS, Beoley Road, c.1905.

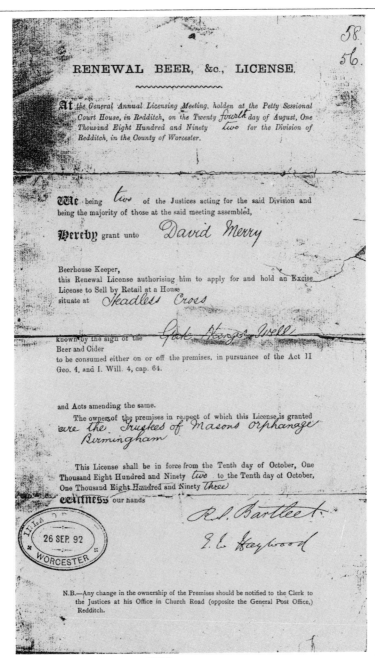

RENEWAL BEER, &c., LICENSE.

58.
56.

At the General Annual Licensing Meeting, holden at the Petty Sessional Court House, in Redditch, on the Twenty *fourth* day of August, One Thousand Eight Hundred and Ninety *two* for the Division of Redditch, in the County of Worcester.

We being *two* of the Justices acting for the said Division and being the majority of those at the said meeting assembled,

Hereby grant unto *David Merry*

Beerhouse Keeper,
this Renewal License authorising him to apply for and hold an Excise License to Sell by Retail at a House situate at *Headless Cross*

known by the sign of the *Gate Hangs Well*
Beer and Cider
to be consumed either on or off the premises, in pursuance of the Act II Geo. 4, and I. Will. 4, cap. 64.

and Acts amending the same.

The owners of the premises in respect of which this License is granted *are the Trustees of Masons Orphanage Birmingham*

This License shall be in force from the Tenth day of October, One Thousand Eight Hundred and Ninety *two* to the Tenth day of October, One Thousand Eight Hundred and Ninety *three*

Witness our hands

R. S. Bartleet

E. C. Haywood

26 SEP. 92
WORCESTER

N.B.—Any change in the ownership of the Premises should be notified to the Clerk to the Justices at his Office in Church Road (opposite the General Post Office,) Redditch.

RENEWAL OF BEER LICENSE, 1892.

LEWIS BROTHERS, PHOTOGRAPHERS, OF ALCESTER STREET were one of the many businesses which advertised on the side of their buildings.

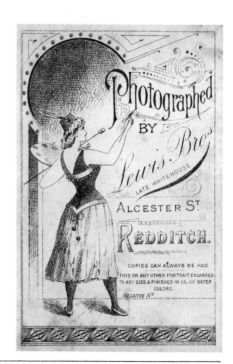

THE REVERSE SIDES OF PHOTOGRAPHS, and this is a typical example, were also used as a means of advertising. These were very decorative and became highly collectable.

THIS GROUP PHOTOGRAPH OF MID TO LATE VICTORIAN TIMES clearly shows the fashions of the day, and is an example of the work of Lewis Brothers.

JAMES BLACKFORD JP, Chairman of Redditch Urban District Council, c.1923.

FOUNDER OF SMITH AND SPENCER LTD, mineral water manufacturers, c.1850. Mr W.H. Smith was also the proprietor of the Hopwood Springs Mineral Water Co. Ltd.

MR JAMES HUINS AND MR SYDNEY LLOYD HUINS, on the left and right respectively, owners of Huins Wholesale and Retail Shoe Merchants, founded in 1796. The shop was on the corner of Market Place and Evesham Street, and known as 'The Boot Metropole'.

MR E.A. HODGES, c.1860, publisher of many of the photographs in this book. His shop was in Evesham Street.

Accept this card and Greeting true,
And let it prove, I think of you.

A RIGHT MERRY XMAS

AN ADVERTISING CHRISTMAS CARD of the early 1900s. Note the telephone number.

POST CARD

FOR ADDRESS ONLY

B. B. LONDON. SERIES Nº X. 90. PRINTED IN GERMANY.

A REMINDER.

That you may require for Christmas. Your Photograph as a dainty Xmas Card, prices from 2/6 per dozen. A Framed Enlargement in Black and White, Sepia or Colors. Private Greeting Christmas and New Year Cards from 1/9 per dozen. Ordinary Christmas and New Year Cards with choice wording. Your Pictures, Photographs, or Paintings suitably framed. Photograph Frames, Framed Pictures, etc., etc.

FOR THE BOYS.

Hobbies' Fretwork Outfits from 1/-, also Fretwood, Saws, etc. The New Strip work Outfits No. 1, 5/-, No. 2, 7/6. These Outfits make an ideal present for young people.

Your orders for any of the above will be appreciated by—

Walter Terry, PHOTOGRAPHER AND FRAME MAKER, **91 Evesham St.,**
(Opposite Council Offices),
TELEPHONE No. 65X. **REDDITCH.**

SECTION THREE

Visits and Events

BAND OF HOPE FESTIVAL, c.1906.

SUMMER FAIR, 1907, with Chipperfields showing a grand list of the latest moving pictures.

TEMPERANCE FESTIVAL PARADE in the summer of 1906 on Church Green and Alcester Street. Note the horse's head advertisement sign on the shop on the right of picture.

THE MEMORIAL PARADE FOR KING EDWARD VII in May 1910 drew crowds of people.

PUPILS OF ST GEORGE'S SCHOOL AND CHURCH in their St George's Day pageant.

ARTILLERY OFF TO CAMP, 1907, at Redditch railway station. A note on the back of this postcard informs us that 'this is Joe in centre behind the dog. He got up early and went to the station to see the local Artillery go off to camp'.

VICTORY PARADE, 1919. The procession is forming outside the offices of Herbert Terry and Sons, Alcester Street.

THE CAST OF *THE MERRIE MEN OF SHERWOOD FOREST*, a production in aid of St George's School Heating Fund, c.1920.

In Aid of St. George's School Central Heating Fund.

"THE MERRIE MEN OF SHERWOOD FOREST."

A PASTORAL PLAY IN THREE ACTS.

PROGRAMME

ACT 1. THE CHASE.

Overture

No.	1.	Recit (Robin Hood)
,,	2.	Solo & Chorus
		"The Huntsman's Horn is sounding"
,,	3.	Recit (Maid Marian)
,,	4.	Aria (Maid Marian) "Sweet Pretty Bird"
,,	5.	Instrumental
,,	6.	Recit (Maid Marian)
,,	7.	Chorus "The Forrester Bold"
,,	8.	Recit (Maid Marian)
,,	9.	Madrigal "Sweet Echo, Sweetest Nymph."

ACT 2. MAY DAY FESTIVITIES

No	10.	Instrumental Introduction
,,	11.	Recit (Friar Tuck)
,,	12.	Wedding March
,,	13.	Chorus
		"Oh Heavenly Father ! Hear our Prayer,,
,,	14.	Song & Duet (Robin Hood & Maid Marian)
		"I'll love thee still"
,,	15.	Bacchanalian Song (Friar Tuck)
		"With a Ho ! Hi ! Ho !"
,,	16.	Country Dance
,,	17.	Chorus "We'll Dance, We'll Sing"

ACT 3. THE CAPTURE & RESCUE
OF WILL SCARLETT.

No	18.	Instrumental Introduction
,,	19.	Recit (Much)
,,	20.	Song (Robin Hood)
		"To Arms, To Arms, the Trumpet sounds"
,,	21.	Chorus "Haste ! to the Rescue"
,,	22.	Solo (Holy Palmer)
,,	23.	Solo (Will Scarlett) "Miserere, Domine"
,,	24.	Dead March
,,	25.	Scaffold Scene

INTERVAL OF 5 MINUTES.

,,	26.	Semi-Chorus of Foresters
,,	27.	Chorus
		"Hurrah ! Away to the Woods, away"
,,	28.	Finale
		"We'll trip it merrily o'er the lea"

CAST

ROBIN HOOD	—	Mr. W. Ladbury
LITTLE JOHN	—	Mr. H. Fowler
MAID MARIAN	—	Miss M. Brewster
FRIAR TUCK	—	Mr. C. Townsend
MUCH, the Miller's Son	—	Mr. H. Chatterley
HOLY PALMER	—	Mr. A. Brewster
WILL SCARLETT	—	Mr. R. Ellins
SHERIFF	—	Mr. A. Bate.

(Chorus of Foresters, Maidens, & Merrie Men.)

Coach — MRS. CHAS. SLATER.

DANCES arranged by MISS D. WRIGHT.

ORCHESTRAL CONDUCTOR — MISS L. HOWES,

PRICE 1D.

Grove Press Redditch.

PROGRAMME for *The Merrie Men of Sherwood Forest.*

B. C. HUCKS, THE FAMOUS AIRMAN, IN THE PILOT'S SEAT OF HIS 70 H.P. BLERIOT MONOPLANE.

Produced by E. O. Hoppe, London.

TWO PIONEER AVIATORS, Benfield C. Hucks and Gustav Hamel, took part in the first air race to fly over the district on Saturday 30 August 1913. The *Birmingham Daily Post* offered a trophy and five hundred pounds a side. The race started at the Tally Ho grounds Edgbaston, and went via Redditch, where the Beoley Road playing fields was one of the landing and staging posts, to Coventry and Tamworth and back via Quinton to Edgbaston. Hamel won the race by 20.4 seconds.

A TYPICAL LOCAL WEDDING, c.1925.

AN ENAMEL BROOCH issued to commemorate the opening of the Royal and Ancient Order of Buffaloes Convalescent Home at Holmwood, Plymouth Road, on 6 August 1923.

THE AVENUE, Holmwood, Plymouth Road, opened as a convalescent home in 1923. In 1965 Holmwood became the headquarters of the New Town Development Corporation. Today the property has been converted into luxury apartments.

SOUVENIR CARD sold at the time of the visit to Redditch on 13 July 1934 of HRH Prince George.

REDDITCH SOCIAL SERVICE COUNCIL

—

The Executive Committee request the pleasure of the company of

Mr & Mrs Harris

on the occasion of the visit of

H.R.H. PRINCE GEORGE

to the

SOCIAL SERVICE CENTRE, PROSPECT HILL

on FRIDAY, the 13th JULY, 1934

Visitors will assemble on the Bowling Green at the rear of the premises not later than 10.20 a.m.

—

It will be necessary to produce this invitation as your authority for admission.

AN INVITATION CARD to the Social Service Centre on the occasion of the visit of HRH Prince George.

DANILO, REDDITCH

GRAND OPENING

SATURDAY, FEBRUARY 6th —— At 7 p.m.
(Doors open at 6-15); by

LADY THROCKMORTON
Supported by G. E. WHITMORE, Esq., J.P.
(Chairman of the Redditch Urban District Council)

Balcony 1/6

Entire proceeds to be devoted to
SMALLWOOD HOSPITAL EXTENSION FUND.

A TICKET FOR THE GRAND OPENING, by Lady Throckmorton, of the Danilo Cinema, 6 February 1936.

16   *Advertisement.*

BOSCO'S PICTURES, LTD.,
PUBLIC HALL, REDDITCH.

ONLY AT BOSCO'S BOSCO'S PICTURES comprise the finest films and screen-plays obtainable—produced by the best cinema actors, with the aid of the latest photographic appliances. Bosco's spare neither pains nor expense to secure the best for their patrons, and often-times, at enormous cost, will purchase the **exclusive rights for this town.** Such pictures therefore can be seen—— **ONLY AT BOSCO'S**

7 | Twice Nightly | 9

Popular Matinees Daily at 3.

TO OUR FRIENDS IN THE COUNTRY When you come into town do not forget the Popular Matinee of Bosco's Pictures at the Public Hall, at 3 p.m., when you will see exactly the same pictures as are shown in the evening.

ADMISSION TO MATINEE | Adults - 5d. and 9d. Children 2d. and 5d.

PLUSH TIP-UP SEATS THROUGHOUT.
SEATS MAY BE BOOKED AND RESERVED.

5D. | Prices of Admission Booked Seats 3d. extra. | 9D.

☞ Every part of the Hall is thoroughly and regularly disinfected by the latest and most scientific methods.

AN ADVERTISEMENT FOR BOSCO'S PICTURES LTD, c.1920. This picture house was in Church Road, and regularly disinfected, as the advert states.

THE BICENTENARY CELEBRATIONS of Henry Milward and Sons Ltd, 1930. Sir Robert Gower congratulates two old employees, Mrs James and Mrs Walton.

ROYAL INTEREST at the British Industries Fair, as HM King George V and Queen Mary examine the stand of Henry Milward and Sons.

LODGE ROAD FLOAT in the Redditch Carnival, believed to be c.1939. The crowded float was awarded third prize.

A 1946 CARNIVAL FLOAT entered by Herbert Terry and Sons.

THIS PLAQUE depicting the story of Flight and Modern Technology was struck in bronze to commemorate the opening of the High Duty Alloys Factory, by Sir Kingsley Wood, the Air Minister in August 1939.

THE ANNUAL INSPECTION OF THE DRUM AND FIFE BAND of the Redditch Company, 2nd Battalion Worcestershire Brigade of Rifle Volunteers, are pictured here around October 1875. These volunteers, the territorials of the Victorian age, were very proud of their green uniforms, but to the locals they were known as 'The Butterfly Shooters', a nickname not favoured by the men.

The Rifle Corps, pictured opposite, had its own song:

Up and arm you, one and all
Arm to guard our native shore,
Sons of Freedom, hear the call –
Arm you, as in days of yore.

Harken not to them that say,
Is not France our true ally?
Never war will come our way;
Lay then, lay the rifle by.

Harken not, but grasp your arms;
They are walls and bulwarks strong;
Let us have no vain alarms,
Tempting France to do us wrong.

Up to guard your country – Arm you;
Find the rifle ev'ry man;
If they say 'We will not harm you',
Make it, 'Neither will nor can.'

A LOCAL FACTORY ANNUAL OUTING, believed to be Herbert Terry and Sons, in the early 1930s, taken at the top of Red Lane on a misty summer morning.

A CYCLE CLUB MEET in Walford Street on 14 April 1906. The chimney of Brown's Brewery can be seen in the background.

CORONATION DAY, 1937, and a party for the children of Lodge Road, Marsden Road and Smallwood Street.

ABBEY MEADOWS. These 'shade trees' were donated to the town by Lady Harriet Windsor. The Bordesley Abbey excavation site can be seen in the background.

SECTION FOUR

The Two World Wars

A PEACE TREAT PARTY for the Workers Committee of Beoley Road and St George's Road, 30 August 1919.

COLLECTION OF FOUR CARDS sold at the Redditch Tank Week, 20 April 1918.

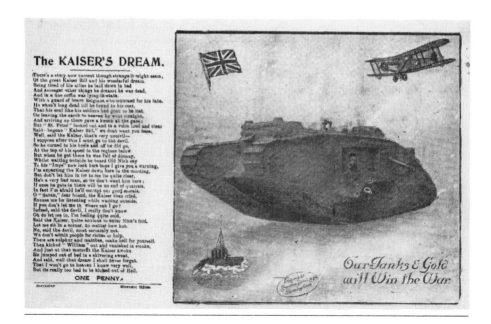

The KAISER'S DREAM.

There's a story now current though strange it might seem,
Of the great Kaiser Bill and his wonderful dream.
Being tired of his allies he laid down in bed
And amongst other things he dreamt he was dead,
And in a fine coffin was lying-in-state.
With a guard of brave Belgians who mourned for his fate.
He wasn't long dead till he found to his cost,
That his soul like his soldiers had gone to be lost.
On leaving the earth to heaven he went straight,
And arriving up there gave a knock at the gate,
But " St. Peter " looked out and in a voice loud and clear
Said - begone " Kaiser Bill," we dont want you here.
Well, said the Kaiser, that's very uncivil—
I suppose after this I must go to the devil.
So he turned to his heels and off he did go,
At the top of his speed to the regions below.
But when he got there he was full of dismay,
Whilst waiting outside he heard Old Nick say
To his "Imps" now look here boys I give you a warning,
I'm expecting the Kaiser down here in the morning.
But don't let him in tot to me its quite clear,
He's a very bad man, so we don't want him here:
If once he gets in there will be no end of quarrels,
In fact I'm afraid he'll corrupt our good morals.
O " Satan," dear friend, the Kaiser then cried,
Excuse me for listening while waiting outside.
If you don't let me in where can I go?
Indeed, said the devil, I really don't know
Oh do let me in, I'm feeling quite cold,
Said the Kaiser, quite anxious to enter Nick's fold.
Let me sit in a corner, no matter how hot.
No, said the devil, most certainly not.
We don't admit people for riches or help,
There are sulphur and matches, make hell for yourself.
Then kicked " William " out and vanished in smoke,
And just at that moment the Kaiser awoke.
He jumped out of bed in a shivering sweat,
And said, well that dream I shall never forget.
That I won't go to heaven I know very well,
But its really too bad to be kicked out of Hell.

ONE PENNY.

Our Tanks & Gold will Win the War.

BRITISH TANK IN ACTION
SMASHING GERMAN DEFENCES.

VALENTINES SERIES
COPYRIGHT

PASSED BY PRESS BUREAU
FOR PUBLICATION 24ᵀᴴ NOV. 1916.

COPYRIGHT E.L.R.C?   ONE OF OUR TANKS   PASSED BY CENSOR

FIFTH BATTALION WORCESTERSHIRE REGIMENT BAND, C.1918, which was comprised mainly of Redditch and District men.

HERBERT TERRY AND SONS SPRING FACTORY HOME GUARD DETACHMENT, c.1943.

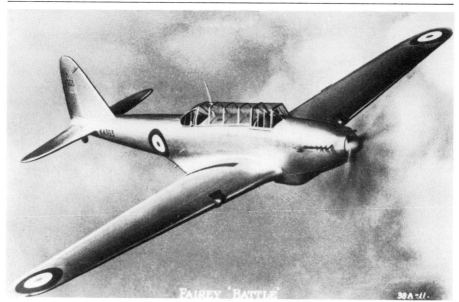

A FAIREY 'BATTLE' FIGHTER/BOMBER built at the beginning of the Second World War at the Austin Aero factory at Longbridge. They were test flown over Redditch, and the golf course in Plymouth Road was one of their practise bomb run areas. From February 1940 the Fairey Battles were flown from the aerodrome at Cofton Hackett to RAF Worcester. Between September 1938 and December 1940 1,229 'Battles' were built at Longbridge.

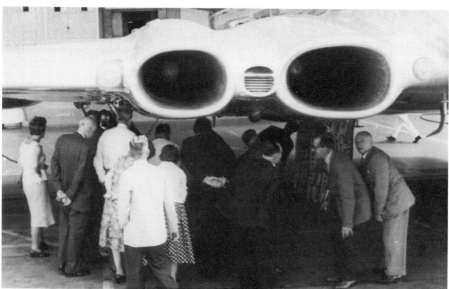

EMPLOYEES OF H. TERRY AND SONS visited the Hatfield factory of the De Havilland Aircraft Company, and inspected one of the first Comet jet airliners.

BRIDLEY MOOR ROAD PARTY to celebrate Victory in Europe, May 1945. The Royal Enfield Cycle Co. canteen and Redditch Gas Works can be seen in the background.

THE RESIDENTS OF MARSDEN ROAD also organized a party to celebrate Victory in Europe, 1945.

THE RESIDENTS OF BRIDLEY MOOR ROAD celebrate the end of the Second World War. It was probably for VJ day in August 1945.

SECTION FIVE

Sport

HERBERT TERRY AND SONS FOOTBALL CLUB, 1919.

REDDITCH FOOTBALL CLUB, 1931/2 season. Players as far as known from left to right include, back row: E. Court, M. Winnit, ? Jeavons, H. Hearne, W. Phillips, N. Thomas, P. Parsons (trainer); front row: W. Rankle, ? Morgan, ? Dunne and W. Leadbetter.

BIRMINGHAM COMBINATION LEAGUE CHAMPIONS, Redditch Football Club, 1932/3 season. Players as far as known from left to right include, back row: ? Morgan, D. Parsons (trainer), M. Winnet, S. Styler, ? Thomas, R. Dickens, W. Phillips; front row: J. Andrews, ? Townsend, ? Jeavons, W. Leadbetter, and R. Michie (manager).

REDDITCH FOOTBALL CLUB, 1925. The team manager R. Michie was a teacher and sports master at St Luke's School, Headless Cross. He is on the extreme right of back row.

S. ALLCOCK AND SONS STANDARD WORKS FOOTBALL CLUB, 1920/1 season.

THE RECREATION GROUND OF BRITANNIA BATTERIES LTD, photographed before 1939. This area is now the site of St Bede's Roman Catholic School, Studley Road.

GOLF LINKS CLUB HOUSE, Plymouth Road, c.1923.

ST GEORGE'S JUNIOR FOOTBALL CLUB.

Crabbs Cross, Hunt End and Headless Cross

EVESHAM ROAD, Crabbs Cross. This is a typical card view of the time, c.1930, published by Chatterleys, a local firm.

CRABBS CROSS INFANTS SCHOOL, 1900. There are twenty-nine children in this class, and some of them look very young.

SOME EAGER PUPILS wait for the gates to be opened at Crabbs Cross Council School.

CRABBS CROSS VILLA FOOTBALL CLUB, 1913/14 season.

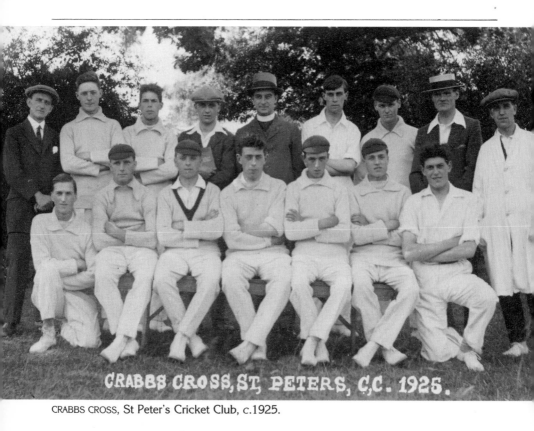

CRABBS CROSS, St Peter's Cricket Club, c.1925.

CRABBS CROSS VILLA FOOTBALL CLUB, 1911/12 season.

THE FLEECE HOTEL, Crabbs Cross, was built in 1897. The landlord during the 1930s, the time of this photograph, was C. Ballinger. C. Whitehouse owned the garage in the background.

ST PETER'S CRICKET CLUB, Crabbs Cross, 1926. Back row, left to right: H. Attwood, -?-, Revd Parrot, -?-. Middle row, left to right: -?-, -?-, W. Jeffs, -?-, A. Batchelor, J. Styler, J. Davis, H. Cund (umpire); front row, left to right: ? Chatterley, P. Chatterley, ? Styler, -?-, -?-, H. Whittington, -?-.

CRABBS CROSS CHURCH LADS BRIGADE FOOTBALL CLUB.

A SIXPENNY TOKEN issued by W. Crawford of the Central Supply Stores, Crabb Cross, in the early 1900s.

HUNT END HAD A FISHERY, before the First World War. The proprietor, W. Crawford, also ran a general store in Crabbs Cross, where presumably he sold very fresh fish.

ENFIELD ROAD, Hunt End, c.1938.

AERIAL VIEW OF THE HUNT END WORKS, 1922. The works were originally built for the Eadie Cycle Co. in the late 1800s. These premises have been used by various famous manufacturers since 1900, notably Enfield Cycles, Britannia Batteries, Dunlop Rubber Co.

A CROWD OF SPECTATORS has gathered to watch the final of the 120 yd race at the Eadie Cycle Company Sports in 1906.

A GREETINGS CARD from Headless Cross, c.1906, and typical of the Edwardian era.

EVESHAM ROAD, Headless Cross, c.1930s, looking towards Redditch. The shop on the right of the picture, A. Bird and Sons, is now a branch of the Midland Bank.

ST LUKE'S CHURCH, Headless Cross. This card was postmarked at the Headless Cross post office on 29 October 1904.

INTERIOR OF ST LUKE'S CHURCH. This card is interesting because it was sent as a Christmas card to Mr Smallwood, of the Smallwood Hospital benefactor family, and is postmarked 8.30 p.m., 25 December 1904.

THE FACTORY OF HEATH SPRING AND NOTION CO. LTD, Birchfield Road, demolished in the late 1980s for housing development.

A THREEPENNY TOKEN issued by James F. Houghton, landlord of the Bristol Inn, Birchfield Road, Headless Cross.

Astwood Bank and Cookhill

ASTWOOD LANE CORNER, c.1910.

HIGH STREET, Astwood Bank.

FECKENHAM ROAD, Astwood Bank.

BAPTIST CHAPEL AND ASTWOOD BANK SCHOOL, c.1910.

EVESHAM ROAD, Astwood Bank, c.1900. This building still houses the bank and post office.

ASTWOOD COURT in the early 1900s.

ASTWOOD BANK FOOTBALL CLUB, 1934. This team was in the Redditch and District League. On the extreme left of the picture is the ex-West Bromwich Albion Player, Ted Perkins.

THE DRIVE, Astwood Bank.

A GENERAL VIEW POSTCARD from before the First World War.

COOKHILL CHURCH, c.1905.

COOKHILL PRIORY, c.1920. King Charles I is reputed to have stayed at this priory on the night of 9 May 1645, on his ill-fated journey to the Battle of Naseby.

SECTION EIGHT

Feckenham and Inkberrow

FECKENHAM CHURCH, c.1910.

BERROW HILL FARM, with the ancient hill site beyond.

BROOK ROAD, Feckenham, looking towards Bradley Green with the Lygon Arms on the left of the picture.

MAIN STREET, Feckenham, and the premises of the publishers of this postcard, c.1905.

INKBERROW CHURCH, c.1913. During the Civil War in 1645, while staying in this area, King Charles I mislaid a map. It is still in the possession of the local diocese and is kept in the Rectory at Inkberrow.

THE OLD WINDMILL, Inkberrow, sometimes known as The Quarry.

SECTION NINE

Beoley

BEOLEY HALL, c.1909.

BEOLEY HALL, c.1903. This hall replaced the house which was razed to the ground during the Civil War in the mid-seventeenth century, and was the home of the Sheldon family.

In Affectionate Remembrance of
JAMES DAVIS,

WHO WAS BRUTALLY MURDERED WHILE IN THE
EXECUTION OF HIS DUTY ON FEBRUARY 28TH, 1885,

AGED 34 YEARS.

A fond and loving husband who was killed in the prime of life,
He little thought when he went out that night would be his last,
Cursed was that cruel hand that caused the fatal wound,
But now laid low to rest in peace in the silent tomb.

A DEATH CARD for Police Constable James Davis. Moses Shrimpton and his lover Jane Morton were charged with the murder of PC Davis, and were hanged at Worcester Prison at 8.00 a.m. on Whit Monday 1885. PC Davis was buried at Beoley church, and a stone known as the 'Policeman's Stone' now marks the spot where he died in Icknield Street.

COTTAGES AT BEOLEY, c.1908.

ST LEONARD'S CHURCH, c.1905.

VIEW OF BEOLEY showing the Village Inn as it was before the First World War — right in the heart of the countryside.

HOLT END, Beoley, c.1904. A very quiet rural scene.

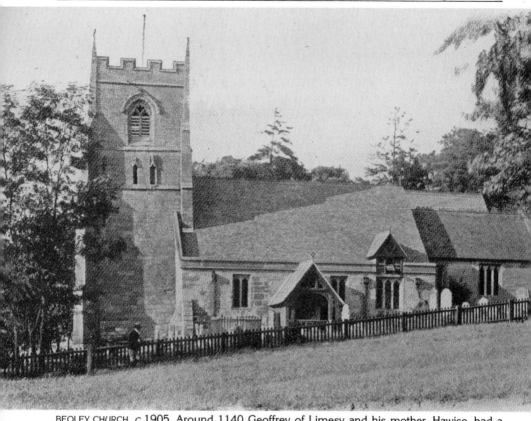

BEOLEY CHURCH, c.1905. Around 1140 Geoffrey of Limesy and his mother, Hawise, had a church built at the top of Beoley Hill. The church was dedicated to St Leonard, the fifth-century patron saint of prisoners.

Foxlydiate, Webheath and Bentley

DARE'S BREWERY, Fox and Goose Inn, Foxlydiate, c. 1928.

THE COTTAGES on the left of this picture, although modernized, are still recognizable in Foxlydiate today.

FOXLYDIATE LANE, Redditch.

FOXLYDIATE HOTEL now stands on this site, where in 1905 people were enjoying the NSPCC fête in the grounds of what was then Foxlydiate House.

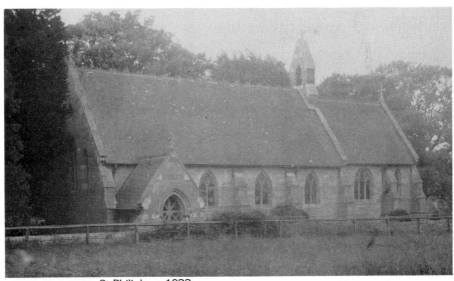

WEBHEATH CHURCH, St Philip's, c. 1922.

BENTLEY BROOK, known locally as the Watersplash, c.1912.

BENTLEY HARRIERS starting from kennels for the Boxing Day meet.

Hewell and Tardebigge

HEWELL GRANGE was the home of the Earls of Plymouth. It is now a Prison Service remand centre.

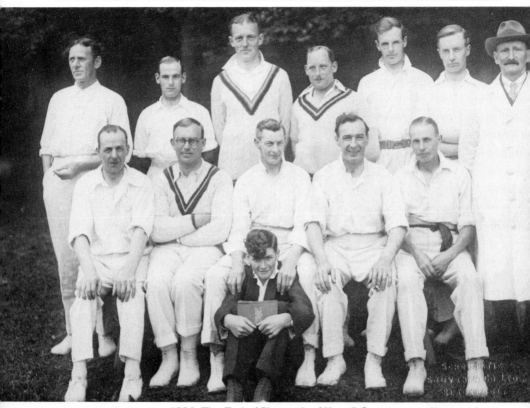

HEWELL CRICKET CLUB, c.1920. The Earl of Plymouth of Hewell Grange was a keen cricketer, and often played in the local team. He can be seen on the far left of the back row.

HEWELL HALL, NEAR REDDITCH.

HEWELL GRANGE, Redditch.

HEWELL GRANGE, Redditch.

TARDEBIGGE CHURCH, 'The Tower on the Hill'.

THE VICARAGE, Tardebigge, c.1920, home of Canon and Mrs Dickens, pictured below. *A Thousand Years in Tardebigge*, the definitive local history book of this area, was written by their daughter, Margaret, in 1930.

NORTH VIEW OF THE TARDEBIGGE TUNNEL on the Worcester and Birmingham Canal, c.1920.

EXPERIMENTAL CANAL LIFT built at Tardebigge on the Worcester and Birmingham Canal. This was never successful and was scrapped after trials.

Alcester

HIGH STREET, Alcester, 1923.

ALCESTER HIGH STREET CORONATION DAY PARTY, 12 May 1937.

STANTONS CYCLE SHOP in Alcester, c.1905.

A.D. HORTON'S CYCLE SHOP in Alcester.

SWAN STREET, Alcester, at the corner of Priory Street looking towards Stratford.

A LOVELY OLD BUILDING on the corner of Malt Mill Lane and Church Street, Alcester, c.1900. Part of the building houses Stantons Cycle Shop.

THE TOWN HALL, Alcester, c. 1923, with a wine and spirit store in the background.

HIGH STREET, Alcester. This photograph must have been taken on an early closing day.

SECTION THIRTEEN

Studley, Mappleborough and Ipsley

AN ARTIST'S IMPRESSION OF THE OLD WASHFORD MILL, c.1730. At that time this was the main manufactory of Henry Milward and Sons.

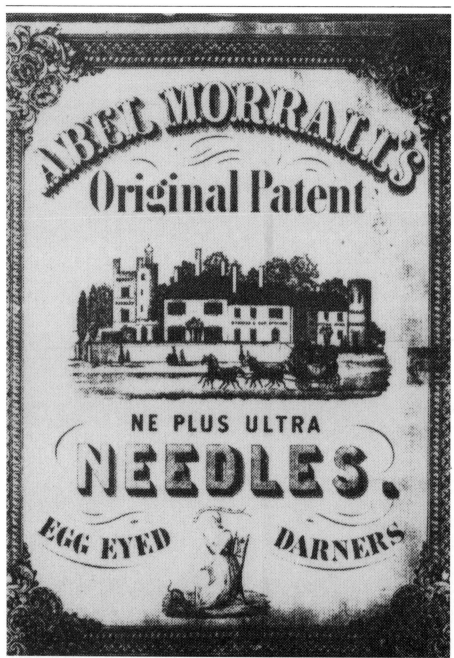

AN EARLY NINETEENTH-CENTURY ADVERTISEMENT FOR ABEL MORRALL NEEDLES, depicting their first factory in Green Lane, Studley, and a stage coach travelling towards Studley.

FLEECE HILL with the grocers shop of J. Hemming and Sons on the left and the Barley Mow public house in the background, c.1920.

THE DUKE OF MARLBOROUGH HOTEL on the right of Alcester Road, Studley. According to the advertisements on the walls of the building it served as a garage among other things.

THE MANOR, Alcester Road, now the headquarters of the Royal Lifesaving Society, UK.

LITTLEWOODS GREEN at the turn of the century. The wagon and horses are thought to belong to George Russell, a well-known local carter and character of the time.

ALCESTER ROAD, Studley.

THE BARLEY MOW HOTEL seems to have changed little over the years.

A GOODS TRAIN on the Redditch–Evesham line near Studley, October 1934.

MAPPLEBOROUGH GREEN. The grocery shop of Hannah Hill at the turn of the century.

IPSLEY MILL AND COURT, once the boyhood home of the poet Walter Savage Landor, and perhaps the inspiration for the following poem:

> I hope in vain to see again
> Ipsley's peninsular domain,
> In youth 'twas there I used to scare
> A whirring bird or scampering hare,
> And leave my book within a nook
> Where alders lean above the brook.

IPSLEY CHURCH, C.1919.

FOXLYDIATE, near Redditch.

ACKNOWLEDGEMENTS

My sincere thanks to Malcolm Barratt, John Brettell, Alan Foxall, Ron and Beryl Smith, Miss K. Harris, Tim and Shirley Ward, Mark and Julie, Alison and Derek, and Bill and Dorothy.

A very special thanks must go to my wife for her patience and understanding, and her help through all the stages of compiling this book.